Into the Shadow

Into the Shadow

A Shadow Work Journal
Mercy Morgana

Ripe Avocado Witch

For anyone looking
to be the best version of themselves.

Into the Shadow

This workbook
belongs to:

_____

An introduction to
Shadow Work

Energy moves in cycles. We ebb and flow with the moon, sometimes we're shrouded in darkness, and other times we experience the beautiful glow. The same is true for ourselves and our emotions. Shadow work can be hard work, but it is necessary for our growth and healing.

The shadow self is everything that we can't see - it's the problems engrained within our subconscious. It consists of primitive, negative human emotions and impulses like rage, envy, greed, selfishness, desire, and the striving for power.

The shadow self is created during our upbringing. Every time an event is met with a bad reaction from someone you deem an authority figure or respectable adult, we push that part of ourselves further down to lock it away, it becomes our shadow.

If we ignore this shadow, it is not only still there, but it acts of its own accord. This is when we have poor reactions to situations and do or say things we regret. These qualities we deny ourselves, we begin to see and attribute to others. We begin to project. If someone does something we don't like, what about ourselves have we swept under the rug? It doesn't mean we are wrong about disliking someone elses behaviour. It means maybe we overreact to that behaviour. There is always a better way of handling situations and shadow work can help.

There are a number of issues that you may experience by keeping your shadow hidden. Some of these issues include: addiction, anxiety, depression, and self sabotage. Shadow work can help you become loving and kind with others, but more importantly with yourself as well.

Working with your shadow can be hard work, but it is deeply rewarding. It can connect you with your intuition and creativity on a much richer level. The goal is to integrate the shadow self and the conscious self to be fully whole.

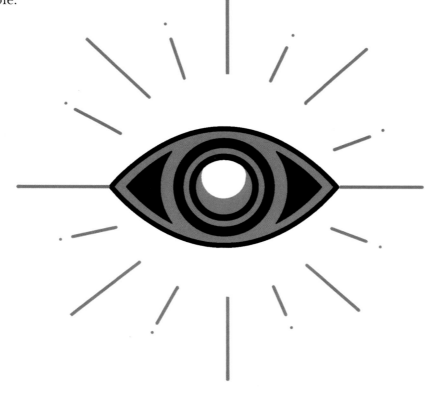

Follow the journal prompts to help discover your inner workings and shine a light on the darkness. For each journal prompt, there is a guide page to help you with your writing.

The goal of the next 30 days is to help you grow, gain a better understanding of yourself and those around you, increase your creativity, and reach higher psychological maturity. If you'd like to get more out of these 30 days, you can try to incorporate mindfulness meditation daily as well.

What happens if you miss a day?

There is a special journal prompt for whenever you miss a day (pg 67). The important part is discovering why you missed a day and the impact that has on your progress. Just know that it is okay, you can always pick up and move on the following day.

The program is 30 days to help change your train of thought. After the 30 days, the goal is that you have a new outlook on life and relationships and you'll be better equipped to handle challenges and stressful situations. It is important to note that this is a lifelong journey, you will find that you will always be able to work on your shadow a bit more.

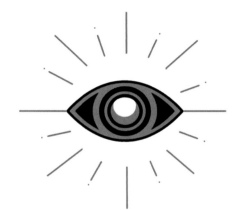

Sometimes we have lingering problems because we view them just as such; problems! Once you've set your mind to treat them that way, it can be easy to be complicit in accepting those issues and working to live around them instead of through them.

With this journal prompt, see these recurring problems as a chance to grow. Whether this is a relationship issue, personal, or workplace doesn't matter. Even if the problem is small, figure out a way to work through it and move on rather than accepting it as a daily barrier.

Example: You are constantly late because your partner takes too long in the shower. Instead of living with this and simply complaining each day, set up some rules for working through it. Maybe you give your partner a time frame, or you get up 10 minutes earlier so you can get into the bathroom first.

Simple problems ask for simple solutions. It just takes focusing on them to get there.

"If anything is worth doing,
do it with all your heart."
- Buddha

Day 1
Date:_____

What are the current and recurring problems in my life?

_____
_____
_____
_____
_____
_____
_____
_____
_____
_____
_____
_____

What would happen if I began to view these problems as opportunities for growth?

_____
_____
_____
_____
_____
_____
_____
_____
_____
_____

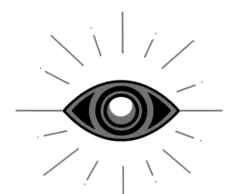

Day 2
Date:_____

There may be many fears that come to mind with this prompt. Let's try to focus on one that comes to mind the most frequently. Working through these fears can help us see that they may not be as bad as a fleeting thought leads us to believe.

Focusing on the fears and turning them into moments of excitement can rewire our brain to a more positive mental state and to have us look toward making future improvements. Viewing the future negatively will only help us remain stagnant in our current state.

Example:
I fear that I won't have the income I'm aiming for.

Your new outlook:
I am excited to finally be making what I think I deserve!

This outlook allows you to feel more inclined to keep working hard toward your goal, rather than feeling like there's no point since you'll never get there. We can't get there unless we want to!

"We cannot change anything until we accept it."

- Carl Jung

Day 2
Date:_____

When I think about my future I fear...

_____
_____
_____
_____
_____
_____
_____
_____
_____
_____
_____
_____
_____

How can I turn this fear into excitement?

_____
_____
_____
_____
_____
_____
_____
_____
_____
_____
_____
_____
_____

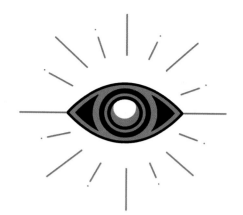

We tend to walk through life with our heads down and let time pass us by. We spend our moments thinking about something we said 3 days ago or something we're worried about 3 days in the future. When we become more mindful, we keep ourselves in the present moment and enjoy life more. We are not in the past, nor in the future, so why does our mind stay there? Minfulness can improve sleep, relieve stress, reduce chronic pain, and so much more.

Example:

TASK:	RITUAL:
- I tend to eat fast because my mind is elsewhere.	- I will begin to think about my food as I chew it. How does it smell? What is the texture? Really enjoy the taste, and savor each bite.

"Act as if what you do makes a difference. It does."
- William James

Day 3
Date:_____

What mundane daily tasks can I turn into mindful rituals?

TASK:	RITUAL:

Day 4
Date:_____

Lots of things can trigger us each day. Sometimes we react poorly (i.e. yelling and screaming when someone cuts us off in traffic), while other times we just let it slide by. The point is, there is always something that gets to us. The point of this prompt is to take a look at the event and reaction and to analyse it in search of the root cause. Why do some people yell at traffic while others don't care? There may be something lurking there that gets you so emotionally charged. Maybe you are self conscious of your own driving. Maybe you know you are going to be late and you are looking for someone else to blame. Or maybe you feel a power struggle, like the person who cut you off may get away with thinking they're better than you.

"The only keeper of your happiness is you. Stop giving people the
power to control your smile, your worth, and your attitude."
- Mandy Hale

⊃ 10 ⊂

"Believe you can and you're
halfway there."
- Theodore Roosevelt

Day 4
Date:_____

One thing that has triggered me today:

_____
_____
_____
_____
_____
_____
_____
_____
_____
_____
_____
_____

What in my past may have led to this reaction?

_____
_____
_____
_____
_____
_____
_____
_____
_____
_____
_____
_____

Day 5
Date:_____

Many of us walk through life on autopilot. Maybe you're living for the weekend. Maybe you are too busy thinking of the future to enjoy the now. Break down the ways you spend your days most and decide whether you are content with this or what about it you would like to change.

Each day is a new opportunity for growth!

"You are never too old to set another goal or to dream a new dream."

- C.S. Lewis

Day 5
Date:_____

How I spend my days is how I spend my life. How does this make me feel?

_____
_____
_____
_____
_____
_____
_____
_____
_____
_____
_____
_____

What can I do to improve this?

_____
_____
_____
_____
_____
_____
_____
_____
_____
_____
_____
_____
_____

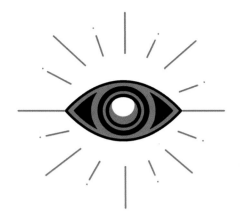

Day 6
Date:_____

We all have those days in which we feel the world watching our every move. How much of what we perceive is actually real though?

Sometimes we only feel judged because we are self conscious of those things ourselves. Have you ever worn a daring outfit and then thought that was all people were noticing? It's more likely that it was just the only thing you could think about. Most people are busy thinking about their own lives and fears, not your outfit.

This prompt serves as a reminder to go easy on yourself and address your own internal judgements before making assumptions about what others may be judging you for.

"You do not find the happy life.
You make it."
- Camilla Kimball

Day 6
Date:_____

How judged do I feel on a daily basis?

_____
_____
_____
_____
_____
_____
_____
_____
_____
_____
_____
_____
_____

How much of that is perceived & how much is real?

_____
_____
_____
_____
_____
_____
_____
_____
_____
_____
_____
_____

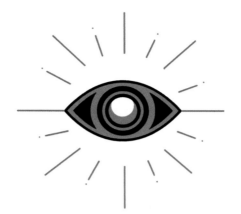

Day 7
Date:_____

Sometimes our isolation is self inflicted. Connect with the reasons you may feel this way and what you can do to either fill the void or better handle a lonely situation. Remember we don't need to fill all our lives with social interactions. Maybe there's a reason you don't want to be alone with yourself.

It's okay to feel lonely sometimes and it's okay to do things on your own. Get to the root of whether this area of your life needs to be filled with people or if it is something you can grow from by going it alone.

"Sometimes you will never know the value of a moment, until it becomes a memory."

- Dr. Seuss

Day 7
Date:_____

Where in my life do I currently feel isolated?

_____
_____
_____
_____
_____
_____
_____
_____
_____
_____
_____
_____

How am I willing to deal with this emotion?

_____
_____
_____
_____
_____
_____
_____
_____
_____
_____
_____
_____

Day 8
Date:_____

We all say and do things we regret later. This usually comes from a deep subpersonality we have. We have many different versions of ourselves deep in our minds, most of which we keep hidden. If we engage these thoughts and behaviours with our conscious mind, we can avoid outbursts from them. The goal is to integrate all parts of ourselves so that the conscious mind is always in control.

Example:
Your friend asked you what you think about their most recent artwork. You thought it was nice, but told them it's not your style instead of complimenting them or giving ligitimate critique. This may have been a part of you reacting out of jealousy - maybe you have been pushing off increasing your art skills and this moment has made a part of you feel threatened.

Day 8

Date:_____

When was the last time I did or said something and then wondered why I did? What happened?

_____
_____
_____
_____
_____
_____
_____
_____
_____
_____
_____
_____

How can I forgive myself and move on?

_____
_____
_____
_____
_____
_____
_____
_____
_____
_____
_____
_____

A look into Archetypes

For days
9, 10, 11, 12, 13

For the next five days, we will be working on different archetypes and their corresponding shadows. An archetype is a typical example of a person or thing. It is a persona that has been stripped to a few core values and packaged in an easily digestible manner for us to use in a comparitive fashion.

Using the archetyps will help to discover the parts of ourselves that are already great and the shadow versions that may be countering and hindering those great behaviours. It's a way to see a part of us that is negative and gives the tools for turning that around.

The five archetypes we will look at are:

The Lover
The King
The Magician
The Warrior
The Caregiver

There are many more archetypes to break down, but these are some of the more core personas. If you enjoy the archetype practice, take what you have learned and apply it to whichever other archetypes interest you.

The Lover

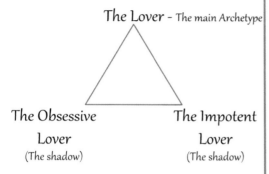

The Lover - The main Archetype

The Obsessive
Lover
(The shadow)

The Impotent
Lover
(The shadow)

Each archetype has two shadow parts that hide themselves deep within us. Today's focus is on The Lover. How we embody the lover is important: do you tell people you love them? Do you look for beauty in all of your conversations and environment?

Or do you let the shadows take over?

The obsessed lover is on a constant hunt for more. The shadow shows itself in those who can't stay faithful, or leaders who abuse the trust of their flock. Or simply showing in those who get lost in work or creative projects.

The impotent lover is one who sees the world in grey. The shadow may show up as someone bored, listless, unable to find passion and motivation in their lives. This may also translate to sexual impotence.

Reflect on how you can better embody the lover - the one who lives with fullness, embracing sensitivity and passion without going overboard. The one who seeks and finds beauty in everything around them.

The Lover

The Lover

The Obsessive
Lover

The Impotent
Lover

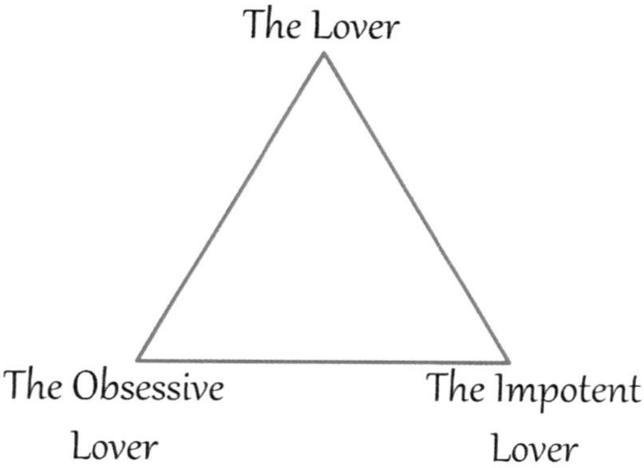

How do I embody the lover archetype daily?

_____
_____
_____
_____
_____
_____
_____

How do the shadow lovers try to take over?

_____
_____
_____
_____
_____
_____
_____
_____

The King

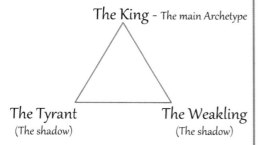

The King - The main Archetype

The Tyrant
(The shadow)

The Weakling
(The shadow)

Today's focus is on The King. The king archetype is the masculine side of us. It is the part of us that is strategic, self-aware, and acts with grace and wisdom. It is the part that has learned the value of wise friends and associates.

And then there are the shadows...

The tyranical king is one plagued by narcissism. Rather than building others up, it seeks to tear things down. This usually includes a scarcity mentality; a belief that power is finite. This shadow tends to lash out with abuse of power or control and hoard things for themselves.

The weakling shadow tends to hand over power, control, and responsability of their own life. This shadow may show by letting others make decisions for them. They may become paranoid that someone is out to get them whenever they are in any position of power.

Reflect on how you can better embody the king and face the shadows. Establish the core values that make you king and protect your traits of true leadership while living with integrity.

The King

The King

The Tyrant   The Weakling

How do I embody the king archetype daily?

_____
_____
_____
_____
_____
_____
_____

How do the shadows try to take over?

_____
_____
_____
_____
_____
_____
_____
_____

The Magician

The Magician - *The main Archetype*

The Manipulator
(The shadow)

The Innocent One
(The shadow)

Today's focus is on The Magician. The magician archetype is wise, thoughtful, reflective, and transformative. The magician is the inventor, the linguist, the mathematician; without this archetype, there is no creation or innovation.

And then there are the shadows...

The detached, manipulative magician may use their knowledge and power to control others. This is done both through lying and withholding information. This can leave you cold, calculating, and cynical.

The denying innocent one plays the opposite role; the helpless victim. This shadow urges you to keep your head down and accept things at face value. It often leaves one evious of others and with a fear that others may discover their lack of responsibility.

Reflect on how you can better embody the magician and how you already create and share information. List your skills and how you share your knowledge with others.

The Magician

The Magician

The Manipulator   The Innocent one

How do I embody the magician archetype daily?

_____
_____
_____
_____
_____
_____
_____

How do the shadows try to take over?

_____
_____
_____
_____
_____
_____
_____

The Warrior

The Warrior - The main Archetype

The Sadist
(The shadow)

The Masochist
(The shadow)

Today's focus is on The Warrior. The warrior archetype is decisive, mindful, adaptable, purposeful, and disciplined. It is what helps us reach for goals, fight for worthy causes, and achieve greatness.

And then there are the shadows...

The sadistic warrior is one detached from their emotions. They may need this outlook for work at times, but they also don't know how to turn it off. This shadow can be cruel and despises weakness. They may choose work over family often.

The masochistic warrior may feel powerless and let others walk all over them. The shadow may make one feel good about being the martyr; remaining in difficult situations just to continue to be trampled on. This could also relate to work - staying in a job you hate, while trying to be the model employee and complaining about it at the same time.

Reflect on how you can better embody the warrior and how you can reach goals in a well rounded way. Think about remaining emotionally whole, not cutting yourself off from feeling and not seeking pity.

The Warrior

The Warrior

The Sadist   The Masochist

How do I embody the warrior archetype daily?

_____
_____
_____
_____
_____
_____
_____

How do the shadows try to take over?

_____
_____
_____
_____
_____
_____
_____
_____

The Caregiver

The Caregiver - The main Archetype

The Victim
(The shadow)

The Slave
(The shadow)

Today's focus is on The Caregiver. The caregiver archetype considers others. It is kind, compassionate, patient, and nurturing. A caregiver is generally easy to get along with, flexible, and able to take good care of themselves as well.

And then there are the shadows...

The victim is the shadow aspect that feels taken advantage of. This can happen by enabling others and not respecting your own boundaries. This shadow may bring about feelings of guilt and inadequacy.

The slave shadow tends to manifest itself as resentment. If the caregiver is giving too much of themselves, they can lose their own persona and feel stuck in their role, submitting only to the person for whom they are caring.

Reflect on how you can better embody the caregiver while respecting your own boundaries and limitations. You are your best self when you are properly taken care of. Once you've cared for yourself, this archetype comes more easily.

The Caregiver

The Caregiver

The Victim   The Slave

How do I embody the caregiver archetype daily?

_____
_____
_____
_____
_____
_____
_____

How do the shadows try to take over?

_____
_____
_____
_____
_____
_____
_____
_____

There are many other archetypes you could look into if you feel you do not resonate with the five discussed. Always look at both the main archetype and its shadow parts to help your reflection and work in embodying the best aspects of each type.

Some others to consider:

The Jester

The Explorer

The Outlaw

The Sage

The Artist

"You must do the things you
think you cannot do."
- Eleanor Roosevelt

Day 14
Date:_____

Reflecting back on the archetypes, which do I feel I embody most? Why?

_____
_____
_____
_____
_____
_____
_____
_____
_____
_____
_____

Which archetypal shadow do I most need to work on?

_____
_____
_____
_____
_____
_____
_____
_____
_____
_____
_____
_____

Day 15
Date:_____

Our pasts stick with us whether we actively reflect or not. This is a major contributor to our overall persona as an adult. It's important to reflect on the situations where we felt we were mistreated or wronged to see how we keep that memory alive now and how we can grow from it instead of lingering in it. These may be instances that have now lead to resentment in adulthood.

For Example:
When you were young, maybe you had an younger sibling who enjoyed disrupting you. They hit you repeatedly and you kept telling them to stop. Getting fed up, you hit back and your younger sibling begins crying. You inevitably get in trouble while your younger sibling is let off the hook.

"It isn't where you came from.
It's where you're going that counts."
- Ella Fitzgerald

Day 15
Date:_____

What is one time I remember feeling wronged as a child?
Why?

_____
_____
_____
_____
_____
_____
_____
_____
_____
_____
_____
_____

How does this affect me still?

_____
_____
_____
_____
_____
_____
_____
_____
_____
_____
_____
_____
_____

Day 16
Date:_____

Envy usually manifests as a result of insecurity and feelings of inadequacy. We may resent others for having things that we only wish to have. This however, can keep us from advancing and getting these things for ourselves. It's important to shine a light on the envy and the reason we feel this way.

Fun Fact:
Schadenfreude is the experience of joy and satisfaction when witnessing someone fail, instead of feeling sympathy. It is usually experienced out of jealousy and gives the feeling that because they failed, you can now succeed. Even if you know that is not the case.

*"It is never too late to be what
you might have been."*
- George Eliot

Day 16
Date:_____

What tends to trigger envy for you?

_____
_____
_____
_____
_____
_____
_____
_____
_____
_____
_____
_____

Why do you think that is?

_____
_____
_____
_____
_____
_____
_____
_____
_____
_____
_____

Day 17
Date:_____

How we handle our own failures can say a lot about how much inner emotional work we still need to do. Your memory of failure can be something small, like forgetting your phone at work. It's about what you perceived to be a failure and why. How we talk to ourselves after this perceived failure is also important.

Reflect on whether or not you berated yourself after the failure and the exact words you used. If we can change our words, our thought patterns will eventually follow.

_____
_____
_____
_____
_____

"Stay close to anything that makes
you glad you are alive."
- Hafez

Day 17
Date:_____

When was the last time I failed, and what was the failure?

_____
_____
_____
_____
_____
_____
_____
_____
_____
_____
_____
_____

With what attitude did I perceive this failure?

_____
_____
_____
_____
_____
_____
_____
_____
_____
_____
_____

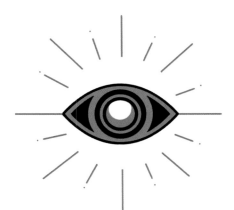

Day 18
Date:_____

We often forget to compliment others as our thoughts are so often turned inward to ourselves. Sometimes, we don't compliment people because we are jealous of their success or we don't want to admit their success. Someone elses success does not equal your failure. It is important to remember that you will feel good when you make others feel good as well.

Sample compliments:
- Admiring someone's creation
- Complimenting someone's work ethic
- Admiring someone's skills
- Letting someone know they are being a good parent/spouse/friend
- Pointing out someone's good idea

*Try to go beyond physical compliments as they tend to not feel as meaningful

"Be the change that you wish to see in the world."

- Mahatma Gandhi

Day 18

Date:_____

When was the last time I complimented someone else?

_____
_____
_____
_____
_____
_____
_____
_____
_____
_____
_____
_____
_____

Do I think I could improve the amount in which I compliment others?

_____
_____
_____
_____
_____
_____
_____
_____
_____
_____
_____
_____

Negative emotions can be challenging to balance. While we don't want to fully unleash the beast when we are angry, it is important to take a step back and view the emotion from your rational, conscious mind. Feel the emotion and what it brings to you, then figure out how to let it go.

Avoiding emotions can be detrimental to our mental health. This is what can lead to unhealthy outbursts at others, ourselves, and at any time.

"Let us make our future now, and let us make our dreams tomorrow's reality."

- Malala Yousafzai

What negative emotions do I tend to avoid?

_____

_____

_____

_____

_____

_____

_____

_____

_____

_____

_____

_____

How can I let myself express them in a healthy way?

_____

_____

_____

_____

_____

_____

_____

_____

_____

_____

_____

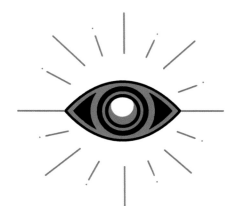

Today we will look at writing a private letter to someone who has frustrated you recently. While writing your private letter, tell this person what it is about them that bothers you, and focus on your feelings around that. Then, let's ask them (ficticiously):

- Why are you doing this to me?
- What do you want from me?
- What can you teach me?
- What are you showing me?

* More work on this tomorrow. For now, reflect on your feelings and the other person's perspective.

Write what you think their answer to these questions might be:

_____
_____
_____
_____
_____
_____
_____
_____
_____
_____
_____
_____

"If I cannot do great things, I can do small things in a great way."
- Martin Luther King Jr.

o the person who has frustrated me the most lately, this is how
u are making me feel:

_____

_____

_____

_____

_____

_____

_____

_____

_____

_____

_____

_____

_____

_____

_____

_____

_____

_____

_____

_____

_____

_____

_____

_____

_____

_____

_____

_____

_____

_____

_____

_____

_____

Day 21
Date:_____

We often feel heavily charged about qualities we dislike in others because we dislike these qualities in ourselves. This is the core of shadow work. Once we can see those qualities match up from person to ourselves, we can not only begin to empathize with them, but we can work on our downfalls and improve. Once we improve, those traits will cause much less strife.

Example I statements:
"I am angry"
"I am jealous"

"My mission in life is not merely to survive, but to thrive."

- Maya Angelou

aking the negative qualities of the person from day 20, and
riting them as 'I' statements, owning them myself sounds like:

_____

_____

_____

_____

_____

_____

_____

_____

_____

_____

_____

_____

ow does this make me feel about traits I may be hiding from
y own view?

_____

_____

_____

_____

_____

_____

_____

_____

_____

_____

_____

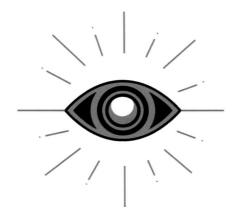

Day 22
Date:_____

Enjoy the things you love in life by figuring out any negative connotations you hold for them as well. Sometimes we feel passionately about something, only to have a nagging feeling of fear or dread along with it.

Pinpointing these fears can help you to better enjoy those moments.

Example:
I love my current exercise routine.
I fear that I could be working harder.

This fear does not serve you and takes away from the overall enjoyment. Notice this and repeat affirmations to counter the thought and retrain your brain.

i.e. My exercise routine is perfect for where I am mentally and physically right now. I feel my best when I engage in my current routine.

"Don't wait. The time will never be just right."
- Napoleon Hill

What do I enjoy most about my life right now?

_____
_____
_____
_____
_____
_____
_____
_____
_____
_____
_____
_____

Do I have any underlying fears surrounding it?

_____
_____
_____
_____
_____
_____
_____
_____
_____
_____
_____
_____
_____

Day 23
Date:_____

First and most importantly, this exercise is in relation to victimization in situations outside of abuse. If you are experiencing any form of abuse, it is not your fault and you should seek help immediately.

With this exercise, think of a moment in which you maybe took a backseat and passively let a situation dissolve in a way that does not suit you. You let yourself feel like the victim of the story, when perhaps you could have stood up for yourself instead. Sometimes we let life happen to us and we play the blame game instead of owning our experiences and moving past them. You have certainly overcome a lot in life and you should be extremely proud! But it's time to start making life happen for you.

For this exercise, think partner arguments, loss of a friendship, a time when you thought, 'bad things happen and will keep happening to me'. A time that you have maybe made excuses for and deny any responsibility for the outcome.

"The bad news is time flies.
The good news is you're the pilot."
- Michael Altshuler

Day 23

Date:_____

id I feel like a victim today or recently? How?

_____
_____
_____
_____
_____
_____
_____
_____
_____
_____
_____
_____
_____

hat role did I play in this?

_____
_____
_____
_____
_____
_____
_____
_____
_____
_____
_____
_____
_____

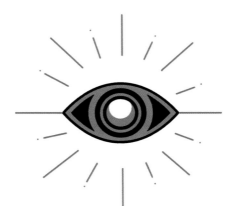

Day 24
Date:_____

Review the journal prompt for today and then return to this page. What would happen if instead of remembering this as a horrible situation, you forgave yourself? What would it feel like to no longer hold the burden of this memory? What if you began to view this moment as simply a small part of a much larger person, one who grew

Reliving embarassing moments can bring up the same mental and physical responses (heavy breathing, quickened heart rate)

and learned from this experience? Reflect on these questions and journal a letter of forgiveness to yourself below:

_____
_____
_____
_____
_____
_____
_____
_____
_____
_____
_____
_____
_____
_____
_____
_____
_____

"If you look at what you have in life, you'll always have more."
- Oprah Winfrey

Day 24
Date:_____

What is an embarrasing memory I cannot shed?

_____
_____
_____
_____
_____
_____
_____
_____
_____
_____
_____
_____

How did I feel in the moment? (mentally, physically)

_____
_____
_____
_____
_____
_____
_____
_____
_____
_____
_____

Day 25
Date:_____

Early memories of shameful experiences can change how we act throughout adulthood. These feelings of shame are usually brought on by a parent, but it could have been an incident at school as well.

Use this exercise to think about those situations and how you may be coping with that experience today. Maybe you had a shameful experience with your body, or food, or your emotional responses.

Don't be affraid to dive deep for this one. Think about this journal prompt as you move about your week and see how the chosen experience is reflected in your decision making. Maybe you hold back doing certain things or saying how you feel.

*"No matter what people tell you,
words and ideas can change the world."
- Robin Williams*

ay 25
ate:_____

what ways do you feel shame in your life?

_____
_____
_____
_____
_____
_____
_____
_____
_____
_____
_____
_____

hat is your earliest shameful memory, and who made you feel
is way?

_____
_____
_____
_____
_____
_____
_____
_____
_____
_____
_____

Day 26
Date:_____

Having and enforcing personal boundaries can help keep us sane and keep our relationships healthy. It can make life easier and reduce conflict. Make sure you have set your own boundaries and are enforcing them appropriately. How can you expect people to respect boundaries that aren't there?

Look at your reactions to those overstepping your boundaries and reflect on how they can be improved. Perhaps you need to be more clear on your boundary. Maybe you forget to restate your position or you allow anger to overcome you.

It can be a powerful thing, walking away from a situation before it escalates and allowing the other person to come to the realization that they have hurt you. Always express your grievances verbally and in a calm manner so that you are well understood.

"Each person must live their
life as a model for others."
- Rosa Parks

ay 26
ate:_____

ow do you enforce boundaries?

_____
_____
_____
_____
_____
_____
_____
_____
_____
_____
_____
_____
_____
_____

'hen was the last time someone overstepped your boundaries
d how did you react?

_____
_____
_____
_____
_____
_____
_____
_____
_____
_____
_____
_____
_____

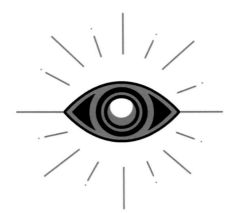

Day 27
Date:_____

Lies we tell ourselves can become too easy to continue. Lying to yourself simply keeps you from growth. There is no benefit for yourself other than perhaps immediate satisfaction that is fleeting. We lie to ourselves to justify or rationalize our behaviour. Once we can see these lies for what they are and dissect them down into the parts of ourselves we are truly unhappy with, we can begin to think anew.

Some Examples:	Possible Solutions:
- My life is harder than everyone elses. - I don't judge people. - I am too busy.	- Get to the bottom of your victim mentallity. - Perhaps you want to feel superior to others - Accept that you do not want to make time for certain things

"Motivation comes from working on things we care about."

- Sheryl Sandberg

ay 27
ate:_____

hat lie am I guilty of telling myself regularly?

_____
_____
_____
_____
_____
_____
_____
_____
_____
_____
_____
_____
_____

ow is this lie inhibiting my overall personal growth?

_____
_____
_____
_____
_____
_____
_____
_____
_____
_____
_____
_____

Day 28
Date:_____

Many of us fear change, whether that change is good or bad, even though our entire nature is built upon change. Get to the root cause of that fear, as it could be holding you back from further changes and from getting the most benefit from those situations.

That doesn't mean all change needs to be seen as good, it means we can accept difficult change better when we are more emotionally equipped to handle it.

Bonus Journal:
How has this change made you a stronger person:
_____
_____
_____
_____
_____
_____

"A man is whole only when he takes
into account his shadow."
- Djuna Barnes

Day 28

Date:_____

When was the last time I experienced a change that upset me?

_____
_____
_____
_____
_____
_____
_____
_____
_____
_____
_____
_____
_____

What illicited this reaction?

_____
_____
_____
_____
_____
_____
_____
_____
_____
_____
_____
_____
_____

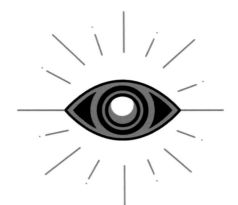

Day 29
Date:_____

Now that you are more familiar with your shadow, let it speak to you untethered. What does it say? Has it been trying to tell you something all along? It is important not to hide this voice from ourselves if we want it to stop controlling our lives.

Bonus Journal:
How can I help this darkness stay in the light?
_____
_____
_____
_____
_____
_____

Bonus Journal:
Who is this darkness hurting?
_____
_____
_____
_____
_____
_____

*"The shadow escapes from the body
like an animal we had been sheltering."*
- Gilles Deleuze

ay 29
ate:_____

a darker part of me were to speak its truth right now, it would
y:

_____
_____
_____
_____
_____
_____
_____
_____
_____
_____
_____
_____

ow does this make me feel?

_____
_____
_____
_____
_____
_____
_____
_____
_____
_____
_____

Day 30
Date:_____

Congratulations! You made it 30 days working on your shadow self. This doesn't mean the hard work is over. Take this time to fully reflect on your experience. Shuffle through your past entries to really dive into what you learned about yourself and how you can use that to grow into who you are fully. Whenever you need a reminder of these shadows and how you would like to work with them, revisit these journal prompts.

In your reflection, you can answer questions like:
- What archetypal shadows did I discover I need to work on?
- What revelations surprised me?
- Who in my life has been most affected by my shadow self?
- How can I continue working on my shadow?
- What aspects of myself am I willing to change?

"If you eliminate my shadows,
I'll be nothing special."
— Lebo Grand

ay 30
ate:_____

hat have I learned about myself from this experience, and how
n I grow from it?

_____
_____
_____
_____
_____
_____
_____
_____
_____
_____
_____
_____
_____
_____
_____
_____
_____
_____
_____
_____
_____
_____
_____
_____
_____
_____
_____
_____

"If you eliminate my shadows,
I'll be nothing special."
- Lebo Grand

Day 30
Date:_____

_____
_____
_____
_____
_____
_____
_____
_____
_____
_____
_____
_____
_____
_____
_____
_____
_____
_____
_____
_____
_____
_____
_____
_____
_____
_____
_____
_____

For missed days
of Journaling

There are a few pages for

missed days,

just in case you miss a few.

"Success is not final, failure is not fatal:
it is the courage to continue that counts."
- Winston Churchill

> **So you missed a day...**

What caused me to miss a day of journaling?

_____
_____
_____
_____
_____
_____
_____
_____
_____
_____
_____
_____
_____

What impact do I think this has on my progress? And how can I keep my commitment going forward?

_____
_____
_____
_____
_____
_____
_____
_____
_____
_____
_____
_____

"Success is not final, failure is not fatal: it is the courage to continue that counts."

- Winston Churchill

So you missed a
day...

What caused me to miss a day of journaling?

_____
_____
_____
_____
_____
_____
_____
_____
_____
_____
_____

What impact do I think this has on my progress? And how can I keep my commitment going forward?

_____
_____
_____
_____
_____
_____
_____
_____
_____
_____
_____
_____

"Success is not final, failure is not fatal: it is the courage to continue that counts."
- Winston Churchill

So you missed
a day...

What caused me to miss a day of journaling?

_____
_____
_____
_____
_____
_____
_____
_____
_____
_____
_____

What impact do I think this has on my progress? And how can I keep my commitment going forward?

_____
_____
_____
_____
_____
_____
_____
_____
_____
_____
_____
_____

If you'd like to continue your work, there are some sample prompts for you below. You can come here and use any as a reflection tool anytime you'd like. You can also re-do any of the journals you have already done, as we are constantly changing and learning.

What triggered me today?

When I think of happiness, what do I see?

How often do I feel anxious? What causes my anxiety?

What emotion have I been trying to avoid lately?

What do I think is my worst trait? How can I fix this?

Thinking back on my last argument with someone, did I try to see the situation from their perspective? If not, how can I see it now?

Follow
@ripeavocadowitch
on Instagram for more prompts!

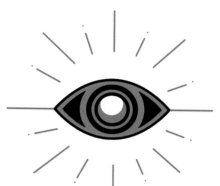

Date:_____

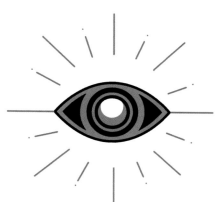

ate:_____

Date:_____

ate:_____

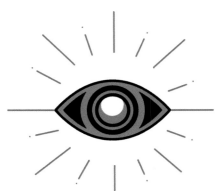

Date:_____

_____
_____
_____
_____
_____
_____
_____
_____
_____
_____
_____
_____
_____
_____
_____
_____
_____
_____
_____
_____
_____
_____
_____
_____
_____
_____
_____
_____
_____
_____
_____
_____
_____
_____

ate:_____

Made in the USA
Las Vegas, NV
30 September 2023

78359251R00052